EBAY

STEP-BY-STEP GUIDE TO MAKING MONEY AND BUILDING A PROFITABLE BUSINESS ON EBAY

BY: GREG ADDISON

Free Bonus: Join Our Book Club and Receive Free Gifts Instantly

Click Below For Your Bonus:
https://success321.leadpages.co/freebodymindsoul/

TABLE OF CONTENTS

INTRODUCTION

Many individuals and families are looking for new ways to bring in money and make a second, or third, income from home. Times are tough, and perhaps you are tired of being gone all day from your family or tired of working so hard and never seeming to get ahead. If you have looked at some of the different options for making that extra income, you can see that a lot of them take too much of your time and effort to work with your current job. But one option that can easily work out with your time constraints is selling on eBay.

Selling on eBay is not something that has to be tough. You simply need to find some items, take good pictures of them and list them and then keep in contact with the potential buyers to answer their questions. eBay has a number of tools that work well for helping you to get your listing on the top of the listing, and you can mix and match things to get the best results.

This guidebook is going to explain all of the different tips and tricks that you need to know in order to get started on selling with eBay. We will discuss the benefits of working with eBay, some of the products that you can consider selling, or how to pick out the right ones if you are unsure, how to get your eBay and PayPal accounts set up, and everything else that you should know to see success.

It does not matter if you've ever sold on eBay in the past or not, this guidebook is going to show you how easy it can be to sell on eBay and make a full time income in no time. So grab this book, find some great items that others would love to use, and get to selling!

CHAPTER ONE
WHAT TO DO BEFORE SELLING ON EBAY?

Selling online is one of the easiest processes that you can try out. Whether you are brand new to the selling world or you have been doing it for some time, there are always a lot of great sites that you can use in order to sell your products and make some money. Lots of people who use these online sites are simply selling their personal belongings to make some extra money or clear out some space, but serious sellers can actually use sites like eBay and Amazon to really make a full time income.

EBay is one of the best sites to use when you want to make some good money on your sales. It is easy to use, has lots of visitors each day, and with all the options in products, it is easy to find a niche of customers who would like to purchase your product.

If you are ready to make a good income with selling on eBay, you may want to get started right away. But before you jump all in, consider these important parts to help you get set up with your account and get ready to sell in no time.

Why should I sell on eBay?

As mentioned, there are quite a few selling sites that are available online. All of them offer some incentives for selling with them rather than with someone else. So with all these options, why would you choose to go with eBay over all the others? Some of the benefits of using eBay, especially if you are one of their members, includes:

- Access to millions of buyers all over the world, making it easier to sell your products.

- Create your own shop on eBay and work to build up the brand of your business.

- eBay's search engine is one of the easiest to be found on as long as you pick the right title and prices. This means that you won't have to spend as much time marketing to sell the products.

- EBay is great for providing protection to the seller.

- You can pick almost any product to sell on eBay, so you won't be limited.

- eBay offers you many ways that you can make changes and customize your products so that it stands out.

- EBay is really easy to work with because there are a lot of opportunities to work on and you can easily grow that online business.

- This site also allows you to test the water. Experiment a bit with prices, products, and even more to find the right choice for you.

- If you would like to support a charity while selling products, eBay makes this easy as well.

If you are just getting started with your own business, eBay is a great site to use. Their process is pretty simple, you can mess around with the prices and the products you want to sell to figure out the best option for you, and there is protection for you as a seller in case you have trouble with your buyer.

Top tasks to do before selling on eBay

While you can choose just to take a few pictures of the product and post it online, this is not the best way to encourage customers to pick your product over another similar option. Some of the tasks that you should do to prepare for selling your items on eBay include:

Sign up for the right accounts.

When you sign up with eBay, you will get an eBay account as well as a PayPal account. PayPal is the easiest way to accept payments on eBay, and since both of these sites are created by the same company, it is a good idea to create a PayPal account that will go with your eBay account.

When you are signing up for PayPal, you will find that the process is easy. You will need to provide some of your personal information and then decide if you would like to set up a business account or a personal account. Since you plan to use eBay to make money, it is best to sign up for the business account. When asked which payment solution you would like to use, choose the standard option; this option is free, and the other options are better for individual websites rather than eBay.

For those who already have a personal PayPal account, you can change it to a business one. Simply go to your account overview and "Upgrade" the account. Stick with the basic package here as well.

Now it is time to register with eBay. To do this, just go onto eBay.com and register; you will see this on the upper left-hand corner. Fill out the form that comes up and then read through the terms and conditions. After you have done these steps, click "Submit." Now that you are logged into an account you will see a "Start Selling," and you will be able to go through the process of registering as a seller. Click on "Sell," and you can start going through the rest of the process for listing your item.

Now that both the eBay and PayPal accounts are set up, it is time to link them together to receive your payments when a customer orders your item. To do this, you will click on the My eBay tab at the menu bar, go to your "Account" page and then look for "PayPal Account" on the left side of the screen. Look for the option and then click on "Link My PayPal Account." Now PayPal should be linked up, and you will start receiving your payments.

Decide what to sell

Once you have PayPal and eBay set up, it is time to do a bit of research and decide what you would like to sell. A good way to practice sell is to get a few items in your home that you would like to get rid of and post them on your eBay site. You can then experiment with what works, such as the types of pictures, the prices, and more. It will help you get some of the reputation you need as a good seller and will expand your experience in this field.

- It is fine just to dive right into selling as well if you don't feel like selling your own items. But you should still make sure that you are picking out the right products that will sell well online. Some options include:

- Find some items that you would like to buy. Chances are someone else would like to buy them as well. Picking out products that you enjoy can make this whole process more enjoyable.

- Visit thrift shops and garage sales—these have some of the best products that you can find. You will find rare items, vintage, items, and more for really low prices. You can then post them on eBay and sell them for a higher price. You can visit a few of these over the weekend and come up with lots of items to sell.

- Check out the popular items list on eBay. This will show you some of the most popular items that buyers are purchasing on eBay at the time. Remember, you don't need to be scared of selling something that is popular on eBay; sure there is some competition, but there are always buyers who are interested.

- Sell complementary items. A good place to start with this is in electronics. For example, you could offer some of the accessories that go with a phone or a tablet and make some good money.

- Sell a personal product—if you already create a homemade product that will follow the policies that eBay set out, you could sell these on the site. This can offer a unique product that no one else has and that the buyer will enjoy.

- Find cheap books—there are some great book sales that go on throughout the country. Finding these and getting a lot of books for a good price can help you out. If they are in good shape, you can sell them as almost new and get a great profit.

You are able to choose any item that you would like to sell on eBay, and many of them are successful. Using this list is just a good way to get started and can make it easier to get those first few sales. Remember that if you find something that is original, hard to find, or one of a kind, and you can get it for a good low price, consider selling that as well. While this is not a crafty kind of site, people still love finding a good deal, and finding something that is one of a kind, and you can make a good return on investment from this.

Check the potential of the product

If you already have an idea of what you would like to sell on this site, make sure to take some time and see if it is actually a good product to work with. eBay makes it easy to check this out. All you need to do is type in the name of the item you want to sell in the search bar. Keep this to just a few words long to make things simple. When you get to the search results, go to the sidebar on the left of the screen. You will see some advanced options, but go down to the section called "Show Only." You will find this at the bottom of the search options, and you will notice that there are three more options, Sold Listings, Completed Listings, Returns Accepted.

Now you will want to click on Sold Listings, and then the results will update to show all of the listings that have sold related to this product. In addition to looking at the prices that this item is selling for, you need to check out the feedback and reputation of the seller, how many items the seller has sold, how the product description was written, if there were good photos, what the title was, and how much they charged for shipping.

The point of looking at all these things is that you will get some good ideas on what you should do to make a sale. When you look at what other sellers with success have done, you get the best ideas to make your listing pop.

Define the purpose of selling on eBay

As with any business that you want to run, you need to have some kind of purpose going on. This may seem a bit silly when you are running your online business, but it is still an important part of getting things to go. When you set a purpose, it is going to help you to stay on the right track. You will have goals, perhaps a purpose in terms of the products that you want to sell, and more. It may take some time to reach your goals, but when you set them out in the beginning, it is easier to see success.

Check your store once a day or more

There are times when some of your customers will ask questions. Other times you may get a few orders and need to complete them quickly to get the best customer service. You don't need to spend all day online waiting for the orders, but when you are posting a new product or doing something else online, make sure that you get onto your account and make sure you aren't missing anything. Remember that with selling anything, good customer service is important to success and being able to check your account and respond quickly will make this easier than ever.

Getting started on eBay may seem complicated, but the process is really easy, and you are going to love how easy it is to sell your products and make a good income in the process. By following the simple steps that are in this guidebook, you will be able to find the right products, start your business, and get your income to start growing.

CHAPTER TWO
THE BASICS OF WORKING WITH EBAY

By this point, you should already have a PayPal and an eBay account set up. If you have never used eBay in the past, there may be some points that are a little hard for you to get down or you may be worried that you will miss out on some of the bonus parts that will help to make your listings stand out from others on the market. In this chapter, we will look at some of the basics of eBay and give you a little tour so that you are able to get started on eBay and have the knowledge that is needed to make some good money.

Essentials of starting on eBay

To get started on this project, you need to get logged onto your account. With your account, you will find that there are a lot of great options that you need to make your listing stand out in reality; you just need to learn how to use them all. Let's take a look at some of the different things that you can do with eBay and how to get started.

How to list a product?

Any page that you are on when you go to eBay will show you a menu bar right at the top. One of these options is "Sell." Any time that you want to sell a product, you just need to click on this tab. Once it is clicked, you will get directed to a new page where you can make the title, listing number, ISBN, or other information that will help to describe what product you will be selling. Luckily, you can access this on any page, so it is easier than ever to get started with selling.

Feedback

On eBay, you will notice that both the sellers and the buyers have the ability to leave some feedback. This is just like with other sites where you will be able to improve your business when you get some great reviews. Customers are going to trust their seller more if they see a lot of positive feedback on the profile, so you need to work hard to get as much positive feedback, and as little negative feedback as possible.

To find where your feedback is, you will just need to look up where your username is on the menu option and place the cursor on top. You will see a drop-down menu and then you will see a star as well as the number of feedbacks your profile has received in parentheses. You can click on this number in order to get to your Feedback Profile. You can then take a look at the feedback previous customers have left for you, comments, and more.

Make sure to check on your feedback often to see where you stand with customers. At times, they may leave some good feedback that you can learn from and make some changes to improve your business.

You can also leave feedback for your buyer. You can go to the item that you sold and there you will see a drop-down menu with the option for Leave Feedback. You will be able to leave a short comment about the buyer and the experience that you had with that process.

Feedback is an important part of how the whole eBay system works. Future buyers of your items are going to take a look at your reviews and see if other customers had a good experience with you. If there are a bunch of negative reviews, you will find that it gets a lot harder to sell items in the future. But with a lot of good reviews, you will be able to get in more buyers because they trust you. Just make sure that you are providing great customer service to help satisfy as many customers as possible.

Seller's summary page

This is a good place for you to start to locate all of your items for sale and other information about you. You simply need to go to "My eBay" and then go to the "Selling" option. When you get to this page, you will be able to see a few different options. Right on the top in the first section will be your Monthly Selling Limits. EBay sets selling limits for new sellers to make sure they learn the rules and so they are able to start setting up their reputation. For example, those who are new to this may only be allowed to sell $5000 in product or 100 products. Over time your limit should go up as long as you are doing a good job with your customers and get good reviews.

Some of the other sections that you can see on your Sellers page include:

- Active selling—this is the section that will show all of the listings that you are currently trying to sell.

- Sold—this section will show you the listings that you have already sold. This can be great for managing feedback, shipping, and other important parts of your orders.

- Returns—this is the section where you will be able to see any returned items in your store.

- Unsold—in some cases, your listing may end without anyone making a purchase. You can check this section to delete the items or relist them.

Selling Totals

While you are on your selling page, you will find a section called Totals on the left-hand side. Some of the details that you will be able to see in the Totals tab include:

- Current listings that are active.

- Sold items

- The number of bids that you have across all your listings

- Listings that are going to sell, such as listings that already have bids from buyers.

- Which items have received payments and which ones have not.

This is the area that you need to check out at least a few times a day in order to keep track of how well your selling is going without having to go into each different listing to learn this information.

When you get started selling on eBay, you need to remember that you will need to pay a little bit in fees to use this website. This helps eBay make some money and can make it easier to maintain the website to work well for this process. If you are worried about the fees cutting into your profit, simply remember how much eBay is going to charge for different types of listings, and then add that price into your selling price. Then the fees are covered, and you still make the full amount that you want. Some of the fees that are associated with eBay that you should know about include:

- Insertion fee—the first fifty listings that you place each month will usually be free. After this time, you will be charged $0.05 for all items for those that fit the video games, music, movies, DVDs, and books. Other categories will be $0.30 each. After you do 100 listings in a month, your insertion fee will just be $0.30 for every listing.

- Final value fee—once you sell the item, eBay is going to take 10 percent of what you receive from the buyer, including the shipping cost and product price.

- Additional fees—there are also some upgrades that you can add to your product, such as subtitles, bold fonts, and more, that eBay will charge you for. Consider whether these are worth your time to pay for.

- Reserve price fee—if you decide to have a reserve price for your auction listings, eBay is going to charge $2 for all prices up to $199.99. If your reserve price is $200 or up, eBay will charge 1 percent up to a $50 maximum.

- 10-day auction listing—if you decide to do an auction listing that lasts 10 days, eBay will charge you $0.40.

- Second category fee—if you want to add an extra category for your item, you will be charged for that second category.

EBay makes it easier to see what your fees will be. You can use the eBay fee calculator in your shop to figure out how much you would have to pay in fees based on your item, the add-ons you would like with your product, and all the other things that will come along. This can help you to determine how much you would need to sell the item for before it goes live so you can add it to the price and not lose all your profit.

Dealing with fees is not something that anyone wants to deal with. This can make the price more expensive, makes it harder to be competitive, or can take out from your own income.

But eBay does need to make some money for updating and keeping the site running. Just remember to calculate this into the price of an item before purchasing to determine if this is worth your time or not.

Getting familiar with your eBay sellers' page can make all the difference in your experience with the site. It can help you to see the various items you are selling, find out if someone has paid you for the item or not, answer communications and so much more. Take at least a few minutes to look over the page and ensure that you are able to find everything that you need to be a successful seller on eBay.

CHAPTER THREE

HOW TO SELL ON EBAY

So far we have taken some time to talk about what eBay is and some of the benefits of using this site to sell some of your personal belongings or to make some good money from making this a full time income. We even took a look at your seller account and how to set one up that is hooked to your PayPal account in order to get started selling products for a profit. Now it is time to post your first item, or items, and get them shown on the site to make the income that you want finally.

Listing Your Items

Now that we have had some time to look at the basics of your seller profile, it is time to get started on actually selling your items. The process of listing your item is going to vary sometimes based on the products you are trying to sell. To do this process, let's say that you are selling a movie.

To start, you will go to the eBay homepage and click "Sell." Log onto your account if you aren't already on the page. Now type in the title of the product, such as the name of the movie you are trying to sell. You can type in the VIN, ISBN, or UPC number to make sure that eBay finds the exact listing.

When eBay recognizes the title of the product, it will show you a list of these products, and you can pick from this. Click on the "Get Started" button or just hit Enter to be sent over to the next part of this listing process. Now you can choose which category you would like the product to be listed under. Under the right category, you will be able to write a good title, look up some tags that will go with the product, and even write out the description to help buyers make the right decision.

Once everything is filled out correctly, take some time to look over the information and see if it is search friendly and looks nice. The product title is really important at this stage because it should have some keywords to help your buyer find it a bit better. You have up to 80 characters to write the title so use it wisely. A two-word title is often not enough to help the customer find you, expand it out to really make it popular in easy to find. For example, instead of just saying kitchen mixer, write Black Kitchen Aid Stand Mixer 5-Quart.

Depending on the category that you choose, there may be a fee to add a subtitle to your listing. Watch for this though because eBay does sometimes offer a free subtitle to sellers, and this can be a really useful way to help the customers. It allows you to add in a bit more information about the product and if you are good about adding in keywords, it can make it easier to have the product show up in search engine results.

Next, you need to tell the customer the condition the item is in. Try to be as honest as possible about this because if you lie and say it is in excellent condition when it is falling apart, you will find that the customers will return the item and they will leave you bad reviews in the process.

Make sure to add pictures of the product you are trying to sell. It is best if you use up all 12 spaces for pictures if you can because this really helps the customers to have a good idea of what the product looks like from all positions and whether it is in the shape that you want. The extra pictures may take some more work, but you will find that it is a great way to ensure that the customer understands what product they are getting and they are more likely to make the purchase.

Filling out the specifics of the item can save you a lot of time. If you only write one or two lines, you are likely to get tons of emails about the products with simple things asked. Many of these messages will lead to no sales, so it is a real waste of time. Consider just filling out the item specifics to save this time and to help the customer out. In addition, make sure to fill out the following text box with more details that you can think of. Of course, there are some items that aren't going to have a ton of things that you can say but fill out as much as possible.

Pricing

Now it is time to move onto pricing your item. The pricing is sometimes going to vary depending on the type of listing that you are working on. There are two types of listings that you can choose from on eBay; buy it now or auction style.

- Auction style—this is the format that you set up so that buyers can place bids on the item. You will set a starting price that you are comfortable with and then buyers can bid from there. The auction style listing also has a reserve price that you can set; this is basically the minimum amount that you will take on the product, and if the bids don't reach the minimum amount, the item is not sold. If the item goes above this price listed, it will go to the highest bidder at the end of the bidding process.

- Buy it now—this is the format that allows the buyer to make a purchase right now without having to place bids or wait for the auction to end. There is also a "Best Offer' option that will go with these listings so a buyer can send over an offer if they don't want to pay the original amount. You can counteroffer this, reject it, or even accept.

When you are working on the price section, eBay will often give you a recommendation for the best price that you should consider setting based on the average price of similar products. You can go with these suggestions if you are just starting out with this process, or you can choose to set a different price you are comfortable with.

After you list the price that you would like to sell the product for, make sure to list the quantity. This is helpful if you have two or more of the product to sell as you won't have to worry about listing each one of them. Then go in and set how long the sale is going to last. For auctions, you will get up to 10 days for the bidding to occur and with Buy it now options, the listing is good until the seller decides to close it.

One way to get people to pick your item over another is to have a worthy cause associated with your account. You can set up your account to donate some of your profits to charity and eBay will take out a certain percentage of your sales after the product is sold.

You will now need to decide how the customer is allowed to pay you when they make a purchase. Most customers like to use PayPal to make their purchases on this site so make sure that your email associated with PayPal is up to date and that PayPal is checked as an acceptable payment option.

Other parts of the listing

It is very unlikely that you are going to sell your products on eBay to someone who is close enough for you just to carry the item to their home. This means that you will be responsible for shipping out the products that your customers order so coming up with the right prices for shipping are important. Take a look online to find out how much shipping will be for the item you are dealing with to avoid overcharging the customer. If you would like, there is the option of "Free Shipping" that you can use to entice customers to choose your shop.

Setting up a return policy is not required on eBay, but it can be a good way to take care of yourself and make sure you aren't dealing with bad customers. You can choose not to take returns at all or only take them within a certain timeframe. Keep in mind that eBay has their own policy, and in some cases, such as putting the wrong information in the listing, you may find that your return policy isn't valid.

Most of the time, sellers will offer a 30-day return policy. This allows the customer enough time to get the product and try it out to see if it will work for their needs before having to send it back. It is also short enough that you won't have to continue dealing with returns a year down the road when the issue is probably more with the buyer than with you.

The last section that you will need to deal with for your listing is the fees. You will need to click on "Continue, " and then eBay will direct you to a review page so that you can see how much you owe right now. You will also be given a list of upgrades that you can choose that will make your listing more visible to customers but will increase your fees. Choose wisely which ones you would like to add to your listing.

Now check to see that all of the categories are filled out correctly for your product. Look for mistakes or things that you may have accidentally missed in your listing. When you are ready, click "List Your Item." And now the item should be present on eBay.

A good thing to do before you go further is to click on your hyperlink (eBay will provide this) and see how the page looks. Is it attractive to the customer and do you think they will choose yours over other sellers? It is always good to make sure that everything looks just right on your page before moving on to the next item you have for sale.

After you have had some time to post up the items that you want to sell, make sure that you check back to your page on a regular basis. This will make it easy to see if your item has been sold or if you have any activity and other important aspects that make it easier to sell your item. Check this a few times a week at a minimum, once a day is best, to help you keep up to date on how your items are doing.

Selling on eBay is a pretty basic process. EBay has made it simple to set up an account as well as to set up your payment method, post a product, and make the sales. As long as you fill out your account and give good descriptions and pictures to go along with your product, you will find that keeping up with your products and making the sales is pretty simple when you have eBay on your side.

CHAPTER FOUR
TOOLS TO MANAGE EBAY BUSINESS

Now with the basics covered, let's shift towards the advanced managing tools. As your business on eBay continues to grow, your listings automatically enhance. Obviously, you will be making more cash, but you need to invest in some managing tools to keep your business professional. EBay provides some tools to manage the selling process like their free Turbo Lister program (it can get your items placed on the site without filling out the slow and troublesome 'Sell an Item' form) and Selling Manager. Selling Manager is a tool that will help to streamline the process of eBay auctions and sales management. It is very simple to use with minimal requirements; you are only required to have a computer with an Internet connection. The basic Selling Manager is free, and it is available when an eBay seller account is made. However, the Selling Manager Pro can be used for a trial period of 30 days, thereafter if you want to continue, you will be charged $15.99 for the subscription on a monthly basis. It saves an enormous amount of time, and you will not regret the fee once you employ it in your business.

Downloading Selling Manager

If you are looking to download your free Selling Manager, follow these guidelines:

- At the top of every eBay page, an eBay navigation bar is found. Click on the site map tab.

- In the center column of the sitemap, click the eBay Selling Manager tab under the Selling Tools heading.

- Go through the information on the selling manager hub page.

- To activate the tool, click on the Subscribe now tab.

You will then be subscribed to a monthly free trial. EBay automatically changes the information for you at the My eBay selling tab. The Selling tab is also changed to Selling Manager. Besides the standard selling manager, the selling manager pro gives you something extra like automatic listings and relisting of products, feedback to buyers, and shipping status. You can click the selling manager tab to view a summary of your auction. The summary page allows viewing all the sales statistics promptly at one place. However, the links to other pages are also incorporated in the selling manager. If you plan to exceed 50 or above transactions at a time, consider using Selling manager pro. It has bulk invoice printing and bulk feedback features which can save you plenty of time. However, you can also avail the facilities of the third party tools to manage your business (explained comprehensively in the upcoming chapters).

Selling Manager Features

Selling manager is a versatile program, the standard version of selling manager empowers you to monitor or automate many of the eBay's time consuming and dreary tasks. Let's study the headings under My eBay views section.

At a Glance

If you are looking to view the information regarding your performance, At a Glance allows you to do that. The data of the sales is presented in the form of a bar chart like the sales for the last 24 hours and sales for the last thirty days etc.

Seller Dashboard Summary

The seller dashboard provides you a mean to check your status on eBay. The dashboard keeps a record of the DSR (detailed seller rating) you get from the purchasers. It keeps you up to date on whether you are complying with the eBay's policy or not, if you have violated any term it is mentioned here. If you are a power seller (will be discussed in the later chapter), you can view your DSR based final value fee discount in addition to your power seller standings. At the bottom of the seller dashboard, a link can be found which takes you to the official dashboard. By clicking it, you will view a page containing the pointers that will make you an excellent seller- both in terms of eBay and the customers. Check this out once a week, but don't get too obsessed. If you are doing the best job you can, there's not much more you can do to change things. If your dashboard points out a flaw with your sales, it is better to evaluate and make necessary changes with your technique once a week.

Listing Activity

Another important tab on the selling manager page is Listing Activity. You will get valuable information regarding your listings activity with even more statistics on the sale. The next sections focus on the activities you can view.

Scheduled listings

On the summary page, the scheduled listings tab is present. It takes you to any auction, fixed-price, or store listing you have placed on eBay which is pending and scheduled for a later time frame. You can also hyperlink your listings here. Whenever the users click on the hyperlinked listings, detailed account of the items can be seen. The URL of the pending listings can be utilized to hyperlink the listings. This page confirms all information about the sale and records every change made to the pending listings.

Active listings

Active listings tab is also present on the Summary page. Just like the My eBay selling page, the identical bidding action is observed even the color coding is same. Your current listings are clickable. The active listings can be categorized on the basis of auctions, fixed-price, or store listings. However, the listings can also be searched for the specific item through their item number.

Ended listings

There is another option for the ended listings which can be accessed from the tabs. Most importantly another tab of prime value is the 'Eligible for Relist fee credit.' This tab directs you to listings for the relisting purpose. eBay refunds initial listing fees if the products sell the second time. Bear in mind, to be eligible for relisting credit; the item gets only one shot at reselling. If the item is relisted twice, you have to initiate the listing again by using the Sell Similar tab. The similar sell tab begins the transaction in a new cycle for the eBay servers, in this manner making it eligible for the relisting credit if it doesn't sell. There is a basic difference between Relisting and Sell Similar. You need to *relist* an item that hasn't sold so you can get a refund on your listing fees if it sells the second time. (This doesn't imply on the third go.) When an item has been sold, you use the Sell Similar tab. That way, if it doesn't sell, you'll be able to relist and take advantage of the possible refund.

Sold listings

The sold listings tab is also embedded in the summary page. This tab makes the selling manager different and appealing. You will find a few additional tabs here:

- **Awaiting payment:** This is where items that have been won or bought are shown before payment is made.

- **Buyers eligible for combined purchases:** When a buyer buys more than one product from you, and you need to consolidate the items into a single invoice, the facility of this tab can be employed. If you are not consolidating the purchases, the buyer may pay you once for each transaction and then you will suffer in the form of extra transaction fees from PayPal. Furthermore, combined purchases help if you want to give your good customers a break on shipping.

- **Awaiting Shipment:** Once a buyer has sent payment through PayPal, the transaction automatically shifts to this heading.

- **Paid and Shipped:** After an item is paid for, a reference to it appears here so you can keep track of the feedback you need to leave.

- **Dispute Console:** This is where you turn in non-paying buyers and file an Unpaid Item Dispute.

My eBay Views links

Selling manager has more tabs on the left side of the My eBay page like Archived item and Unsold items. The archived tab contains the information of the products that had been closed within the last four months. This data can be downloaded on your computer, and it is better to preserve it for record maintaining purposes. Moreover, the unsold tab can be used to relist the items.

Seller tools links

You will also find a seller tool box on the summary page. This tool box consists of a group of exciting facilities like quick links to PayPal, Accounting assistant, Picture manager, My eBay store, and the old My eBay selling page (the one which is seen before the selling manager pro is subscribed). In addition, your sales history can be downloaded to your computer.

Manage My Store

If you have an eBay store (details will be discussed in a separate chapter), you will see a tab with all the options that you need to manage the store. Some of the options are access e-mail marketing tools, markdown manager, reports, etc.

Auto-Sending Invoices

One of the most promising features of selling manager is that it allows you to view the progress of your sales from the summary page. When an item is won or paid for utilizing PayPal, it can be clicked to see the list of items ready for an action such as shipping. A reference record number is placed adjacent to the winner's e-mail address. Follow these guidelines to send an e-mail or invoice to the customer.

On clicking the reference number placed adjacent to the customer's email address the sales record for that particular transaction pops up. The items purchased by the customer are mentioned along with their serial number. If the customers have purchased more than one item, you can consolidate these purchases to make a single invoice. Then click on the e-mail option, and select a suitable e-mail template. You can always customize the e-mail templates supplied by the selling manager according to your likings. This is to give a more personal touch to the e-mail, and the customers like to be treated well. When all the requirements are met, simply send the e-mail.

Tracking Payments

Selling manager makes sale process streamlined. Take a look at your selling manager summary page. You can view the buyers who have paid for their purchases, and the buyers who haven't paid are also enlisted. If you are expecting payments, make sure that you check the summary page several times a day. When a buyer makes his/her purchase through PayPal, selling manager automatically updates your status. PayPal also sends a confirmatory e-mail about the payment received, but it is usually delayed.

After shipping the item, make sure to mention it on the sales status and notes screen. The transaction information can be retrieved when the record number adjacent to the shipped item is clicked. Once you have shipped the item, provided the relevant information, and saved the proceedings, the records will be shifted to Paid and Shipped page. Recently, the information was stored in the sold listings under the Paid and Ready to Ship tab.

Relisting

Relisting the items one by one can turn out to be a nightmare; it is an extremely hectic task. If you are looking to speed up the listing process, selling manager can help you in this respect. The whole bunch of products is selected and relisted together with a single click. Follow these steps to relist an item through selling manager.

First, go to the unsold items listings tab available on the summary page. Then select the items to relist by marking the check box adjacent to each item's title. Click the relist button, and review all the items along with their fees. Finally, submit the items by clicking the Submit listing option.

Selling manager reports

This feature keeps all the selling information in one place. It also provides a downloadable report. The statistics are recorded in the spreadsheet format that can be stored for record maintaining. The reports may contain the following data:

- **Sales record number:** The Selling Manager allocates a number to the contract for identification purposes. This is called the sales record number.

- **User ID:** The eBay's user ID of the individual who bought the product from you.

- **Buyer zip:** The customer's ZIP code.

- **State:** The state the buyer lives in.

- **Buyer country:** The country your buyer resides in.

- **Item number:** The eBay's allocated reference number to the item when you listed it for sale on the site.

- **Item title:** The title of the listing as mentioned on eBay.

- **Quantity:** The number of items purchased in the transaction.

- **Sale price:** The final selling price of the item.

- **Shipping amount:** The amount you charged for shipping the item.

- **Shipping insurance:** In case the customer paid insurance, it's listed next to their sales record.

- **State sales tax:** The selling Manager can be structured to compute sales tax for your in-state sales. If sales tax was pertinent to the item when it was sold, that amount is registered here.

- **Total price:** The GSA (gross sales amount) for the transaction.

- **Payment method:** This column contains the method of payment employed by the customer. This is entered mechanically if the item is paid through PayPal, if any other method except PayPal is employed, the method should be manually inserted.

- **Sale date:** The date the transaction occurred on eBay.

- **Check out:** The date of check out. This is usually the same as the transaction date.

- **Paid on date:** It shows the date on which the customer paid for the item.

- **Shipped on date:** The shipping date you submitted manually in Selling Manager.

- **Feedback left:** This column simply indicates in Yes or No whether you have left the feedback to a particular customer or not.

- **Feedback received:** The feedback rating left for you by the customer. It could be positive, negative, or neutral depending on your experience with the customer.

- **Additional Notes:** If you have inserted any additional (personal) notes regarding any specific transactions, they are present in this column.

Remember the selling manager reports are available only for a limited amount of time, usually four months or so. Ensure that you download your information periodically so that you don't miss to record the useful statistics. You should have noticed that the report lacks the eBay fees column that you paid for listing and selling the items. If you manage to find some time, you can create a discrete column containing the eBay fee for each item you paid. An enormous amount of time can be saved if the monthly total is entered into the accounting software regularly at the end of the month. Follow these guidelines if you are looking to download a file to your computer.

On the selling manager page, you will find a file management center tab under the seller tools headings. Then click on create a download request link. Select the listings and records you want to download from the drop-down menu. Your e-mail address is already filled in, but you can add another e-mail if you want a facsimile statement. Select the appropriate time frame for the reports generation. It's best to produce monthly or quarterly reports so that your reports overlap with specific tax periods. You can also merge more than one report in your spreadsheet program to cover different time frames. Then hit the save option, and you will see a confirmation page bearing a confirmation number for your application. eBay immediately sends you an e-mail on the completion of the process. Click on the link incorporated within the e-mail, and you will be directed to view the completed downloads page, now simply download this file on your computer.

The downloaded file can be renamed so that it truly reflects month and year. Later on, when you are trying to find some data, it will be much easier for you to get the information when saved according to month and year. Furthermore, create a directory on your computer with the name such as eBay sales statistics. All the reports from eBay, PayPal, or any other online service should be stored in this directory.

Studying your statistics

Keeping track of the sales statistics is a necessity. We will discuss eBay's store traffic reports, eBay sales reports plus, and an online service by the name of ViewTracker. eBay sales reports plus and store traffic reports are free with the eBay store. The information these tools provide is important for your sales efforts, and most importantly it doesn't invade the privacy of the customers. For instance, ViewTracker may find out the timeslots and keywords used by the visitors, but you find nothing about the individuals who performed those actions. The information service presented in this section doesn't turn your computer into a data mining robot. It solely supplies you the information available to every Web site on the Internet. In simple words, it gives you information such as geographic location, which follows the IP address of all eBay users who visit your listings. This service is not an invasion of privacy like the data mining cookies that are fed into the user's computer to track their searches. Now let's study these tools individually in detail.

eBay Sales Reports Plus

If you are looking to track and record your sales in one place, eBay's sales reports plus is probably the best tool. You don't need to download the sales file, and then assemble them on your spreadsheet. This tool automatically creates files for you. The reports can be viewed anytime from the My eBay page. The following information is provided by the sales reports.

- **Cumulative sales:** The total revenue generated by sales of your products by month.

- **Monthly sales growth:** The percentage of increase (or decrease) of your gross revenue from month to month. It may also be viewed from week to week.

- **Ended listings:** The total number of listings finalized during the month.

- **Ended items:** The number of items represented in your ended listings. Store and fixed-price listings usually represent multiple quantities.

- **Successful items number:** The total number of listings that ended with a buyer.

- **Percentage of Successful items:** The percent of items that sold in your successful listings.

- **Average sale price per item:** The average of the total revenue generated by your sold items.

- **Total buyers:** The total number of winning buyers that purchased items from you.

- **Unique buyers:** The total of unique (specific identification) buyers that purchased from you. If a buyer purchased several items from you over the month, they are counted only once in this figure.

- **The percentage of repeat buyers:** The percentage of buyers who purchased more than once within the time specific time frame.

Although eBay provides you with the data on fees whether on the listings or the final value fees, but sometimes the seller's profit is greatly affected by these fees. Therefore it is essential to keep track of the fees associated with different things at one place. This tool supplies you with eBay and PayPal fees separately, but unfortunately, you have to calculate the fees as the percentage of your sales on your own. Don't worry; it's not difficult at all. Simply add the eBay and PayPal fees and divide them with total sales. Then multiply the answer with 100 to get a percentage. The formula is, Fee percentage = (net eBay + PayPal fees/total sales)* 100. You can also see how many unpaid item reminders you filed, the number of final value fee discounts you claimed, and the percentage of unpaid items as a percentage of your sales. The data accumulated can be seen separately with respect to auctions, fixed price sales, and store items. You can also see which days of the week were most profitable for you, and the data is represented in the chart format.

ViewTracker

Sellathon's ViewTracker is another tool that will help to maintain your sales record. An enormous amount of time was spent to research the customer habits and timings of shopping. When trying to estimate the exact time and date to end an auction, people had to run test auctions on the eBay site. But ViewTracker has put a full stop to the misery. Now you can follow the body clocks of your customers and figure out when they search items relevant to yours. Furthermore, you can also get the data about the keywords that the customers used to find your listings. This information can be used when putting on the titles and descriptions of your listings. You may wonder what else ViewTracker provide? Let's look some of the data types you may collect:

- You can get the sequential number of the visitor. That means is it the 5th visitor or 120th visitor? You can also find out the visit of that person (visitor) again.

- The exact date and time the visitor sneaked at your auction.

- Visitor's IP address (you don't get the complete IP address, but if the surfer has repeated visits it is recorded).

- A question mark is present, and if you click the question mark, a window pops up that show the city, state, and country of the visitor.

- What was the status of the reserved price when the visitor arrived?

- How many people have been placed to that moment when the item received a bid? Also, the timing of the bid is mentioned.

- The potential of the visitor (whether a high bidder, out bidder, or not a valid bidder).

- Has the visitor chosen to watch the listings from their My eBay page?

- How did the visitor reach your listings? Whether they browsed a category, searched through a specific category or all of eBay listings, used eBay's product finder utility, or reached from See Seller's other Items Page or some other source.

- If they were browsing, which category were they browsing when they finally reached your listings?

- In case they were searching, what keyword did they use?

- If searching, were they matched from the titles of your listings, descriptions, or both of them?

- Whether the surfer opted to view the auctions, buy it now, or both.

- Whether the surfers used any specific parameters to limit their search results. If yes, were that show/hide pictures, sellers that permit PayPal transactions, Price window, international shipping, regional searching, gallery view, or show gift items.

- The preferences of the users while searching. Did they sort their search result? Were the products sorted from high to low or low to high?

Isn't that wonderful? With the help of these kinds of data, you can alter your marketing strategy to become more targeted; you will get the more qualified audience. Making an account on Sellathon is a straightforward task. After you have made an account, they will provide you with a code that needs to be incorporated within your product listings descriptions.

ViewTracker's Interface

When you log into ViewTracker, you will be directed to your general items page. Remember the ViewTracker constantly tracks your items in real time, so the data is upgraded at the moment you do alteration with your listings. You will see a screenshot of current sales activity, and a graph representing your views for the past 24 hours. In addition, the home page also supplies you with remarkable data such as the cumulative value of the bids placed on your auctions, the number of surfers watching your items, average visits per auction, the total number of clicks on your listings, and a listing of your live and expired auctions.

A chart representing the trend followed by people to reach your auctions is of prime importance. This chart can be used as a reference to see your marketing sales effort working or not. Your individual marketing plans are also cross checked. Obviously, you need more people to reach your listings, especially potential buyers to give your business an uplift. To make sure, see whether you are taking full advantage of targeting your cross-promotions and if your website is directing the audience to your listings. Study this chart on a daily basis as it may alter your marketing tactics. Another chart of value is the top search terms or keywords used to find your items. This chart will help you to include the most relevant keywords in the titles and descriptions of your listings.

CHAPTER FIVE

MANAGING YOUR EBAY BUSINESS WITH THIRD-PARTY TOOLS

EBay's associated tools have been discussed in the previous chapter. You should be aware of the importance of the managing tools by now. When the business starts to increase many folds, the need for managing tools becomes a necessity. When things become difficult to manage, you can get supplementary help from third-party software. The choice of selecting an online service or residing software on your computer depends on you. You may find an online service more appealing as it provides you the ease of using it anywhere from any computer, but sometimes the slow internet connection or pay usage fees can spoil the party; therefore making the idea unfeasible. On the other hand, many desktop based software allow you to work offline, and then upload or download data when you go online. You may find this better if you work from a single computer. In either case, if your business has reached the level where you need an auction management tool, this chapter will guide you throughout. You will get to know some of the service providers with their details and price comparisons.

Choosing an Auction Management tool

You will find several auction management services and software on the internet. Selecting one of them might trouble you. Nevertheless, the online services offer two important features. First is the uptime reliability. Uptime is important here; you don't want the server that holds your images and miss-launches your auctions. The second important consideration is the software that is continuously matching the eBay's changes.

Placing your auctions through services and software is a whole new experience. Therefore, before buying a software, it is recommended to use their free trial to get a better understanding of their working. Some software and services can be subscribed on a monthly basis while others can be bought in a single payment.

There is a clear difference between auction listing and auction management software. The Turbo Lister comes under the heading of the listing tool, and selling manager comes under the management tool. Many sellers are contented with these two tools. But if your business activity is increased and you turn to an auction management tool, you should look for something extra. Never choose a software on the sole basis of price. Some of them might be expensive, but they may contain some additional features. So look thoroughly before making a decision about a purchase.

Standard Features

If you are looking to evaluate an auction management tool, make sure they possess the following features. These features must be included in the software or service.

Image hosting: Some Web sites astonish you with high-megabyte storage capability. But you don't really need that enormous amount of storage. Keep one thing in mind, as a rule, if your average eBay image is around 50 Kb, you could store almost 80 images in a 4MB storage space and about 2000 images in a 100MB storage space. Unless you're a big-time seller, you really don't need that much space. Your eBay images should be archived on your computer. Images for current listings should be on the hosted site server only while the transaction is in progress. After the buyer has purchased the item, you can remove the images from the remote server.

Designing listings: Most of the software provide a wide range of listing functions. You can select either from the predesigned templates or your own customized templates. The templates can be stored for future use also. Another fascinating addition is the spell checker tool box. You can't afford a spelling mistake in your listings.

Placing listings: Most products have the capability to enlist multiple products on eBay at once. You can also schedule auctions to start at a specific time. The listings can also be arranged offline and then taken up by the service when you go online. All your listings are automatically stored in archives so you can relist them easily in future. Many of them also offer bulk relisting.

E-mail management: You can expect to be supplied with sample e-mail letters (templates) that can be customized to give your own look and feel. The services should also offer automatically generated e-mails for End of Auction, payment received, and shipping.

Feedback automation: Post feedback in bulk to a number of your completed listings, or leave predesigned feedback for each, one by one. Some products support automatic positive feedback that kicks in when a buyer leaves you positive feedback.

Sales reports: Some services (even the least expensive) offer you some sort of sales analysis. Be sure to take into account how much you really need this feature, basing your estimate on data that you may already receive from PayPal and eBay Stores.

Advanced Features

Besides these standard features, you may also require some advanced features depending on the nature of your business. The advanced features could be:

Merchandise tools: The services could provide you with the merchandise records. You simply enlist the items you are going to sell, and the items are automatically deducted if they are purchased. This will provide you details on your inventory and the products that are still not purchased.

Sales tax tracking and invoicing: Sales tax calculation is a serious pain. But with advanced management tools you can relax as they invoice the sales tax automatically. Additionally, if more than one products are bought by the customer, they are also invoiced as combined.

Batch tracking: If you are a trading assistant (selling products for someone else), it is better to find a service that tracks the batch of labeled products separately. This is because you need to record their statistics distinctly.

Shipping: Most of the services allow you to print your packing lists and shipping details directly from their software. While some of the bigger services are contracted with the shipper sites, and you have to ship your items using their software.

Online Auction Management tools

An online service will suit you if you are going to run your business from multiple computers. Online auction management tools cater almost every aspect of your auctions starting from inventory management to label printing. There are many choices available, but we will discuss some of the services here. When choosing a service, make sure the service provider is an eBay certified developer, preferred solution provider, or API (Application programming interface) license holder. These service providers are in direct contact with eBay marketing officials, so they match up and implement the eBay changes immediately. On the other hand, others may take some time to update their respective software. You simply can't afford a delay in business, therefore, select the service wisely.

ChannelAdvisor

ChannelAdvisor is a very popular management service that has the capacity to satisfy almost every eBay seller. They offer two levels of software viz. the MarketplaceAdvisor premium for midsized to large businesses and power sellers, and

MarketplaceAdvisor for small businesses and individual use. This software will help to manage and automate the sale of your inventory. Some of the salient features of the software for small businesses and individuals are:

Listing design and launch: You can create your listings with their predesigned templates or use your own HTML to design auction descriptions. The listings can be scheduled for future launching, and they will launch automatically on the specified time.

Inventory management: In case you need to alter your listings online, you can keep them on the MarketplaceAdvisor system. On the contrary, if you want to work offline, you can download that on your computer. The open auctions and store listings can be imported to your ChannelAdvisor account for relisting or other services.

Image hosting: They supply some space on their server to host images. You can host a limited amount of images at a time, but it can be increased if you employ an FTP to upload a large quantity.

Post auction management: After a customer wins an auction, automated email invoices are generated which can be sent directly to the buyers. You can also print the mailing labels too.

Vendio

Vendio has served more than a million sellers, and they are still in the business. Their wide range of options and features make them competitive and unique as well. Here are a few features of their auction management software:

Item and inventory management: Keep track of your items and launch the listings with a mere click from their site.

Image hosting: For eBay auctions, image hosting is dependent upon your needs at that particular time.

Auction reporting: Creates reports for accounts receivable, item history, and post-sales. These reports contain views that are customizable to your sales data, item and auction data, accounts receivable, and sales tax.

Templates and listing: Provide you with an array of templates. You can use their predefined color templates or use your own customized templates.

Post-auction management: Sends out automated e-mail to your winners, directing them to your own branded checkout page containing your payment methods and details. They also merge multiple wins for shipping and invoicing. You have the option to choose from different feedback comments (templates). Vendio offers a fully customizable Store with no additional charges. When you set up yours, all your items are effortlessly integrated.

Meridian

Another great service is Meridian. Some of their salient features are:

Item and inventory management: Offers date and time scheduling of your listings, automated auction launching and relisting, the ability to import the past or current auctions, and the capability to import auction data from a spreadsheet or database.

Image hosting: Supplies sufficient space for storing pictures. You can upload bulk images to its Web site or FTP your images directly.

Auction reporting: Generates current running auction statistics such as the total number and amount of current and past auctions. An itemized report of each auction is also presented.

Post-auction management: Allows you to send a variety of customized e-mails to winners and nonpaying bidders. Emails could be manual or automatic. Your invoices can link directly to PayPal.

Consignment tools: For sellers who sell for others, the service offers complete tracking and inventory by the consignor. Like many other service providers, you can also send automated feedback and create mailing labels for each sale. The feedback isn't forwarded until you're sure the transaction is successfully completed, you are free to deactivate the automatic feedback feature.

Offline Auction Management tools

Offline auction management services are suited to people who work from their personal computer. Simply a software will be downloaded on your computer, and you can manage all your tasks from there. Most importantly almost every task can be performed by the downloadable software just like the online management tools. Let's look at these tools separately. Following are some of the leading products.

Auction Wizard 2000

Auction Wizard is an amazing offline software developed in 1999. The more advanced version was made in 2000, and it is very helpful even now. Some of its special features include the handling of consignment sales, editing (crop, rotate, and resize) of images prior to uploading, and uploading pictures with built-in FTP software. All data associated with consignments is organized and recorded by the software. The FTP software eliminates the need for other auction business software.

The program's interface is user-friendly. They offer a 60-day free trial. To begin using the software, simply download your current eBay auctions directly into the program. When your auctions close, send customized e-mails (the program fills in the auction information) and manage all your post auction tasks. Some sellers launch their auctions using Turbo Lister and then retrieve them and handle the post-auction management with Auction Wizard 2000.

What else to automate?

Millions of people visit eBay every day, and it has grown to a supreme level. To match your competition, you should react fast. That is you need to post your auctions promptly and accurately. You can't do each and everything on your own. That is why it is necessary to automate some functions to add speed and accuracy to your business. Post auctions, record maintenance, cataloging inventory, managing pictures, and accumulating statistics are all tasks that can be automated. Then what are you waiting for? The more your business grow, the things become more chaotic. Automated tools can help to eliminate this chaos, and your tasks will become more arranged and organized. But with more paid tools, your expenses are increasing too. So keep your price range in mind when evaluating a software and service. Now let's discuss some of the chores you can automate in detail.

Setting up an auction photo gallery

If you still haven't opened an eBay store, setting up a photo gallery is an amazing alternative. The auction photo gallery empowers the customers to view the process of the auction through photographs, in case they have a high-speed internet connection. Some services and software can host your gallery on their server. They may charge you for it, while some other may perform the same function without the fee. But you can also create your own gallery on eBay without the assistance of any software or service for free. Your own gallery can be created with three simple steps.

First, include eBay gallery photos along with all the listings you want to display in your gallery and type in your username in the text of your item's description. Next place the following URL in your browser, http://shop.ebay.com/merchant/*yourUserID.* Place your user ID at the end of the URL. This will take you to your gallery. Finally insert the following HTML into your auction to incorporate a link to your gallery, <a href="http://shop.ebay.com/merchant/*yourUserID*"><B>Click <I>here</I> to view *YourUserID* Gallery</B></a >

You can also add this HTML in your emails to customers so that they find what's for sale at that time.

Sorting auction email

As discussed previously, almost every service and software include the feature of automatic emails to auction winners. When an individual wins an auction on your listings, you simply download the winner information from eBay. As soon as you download the information, this software generates automatic emails containing the invoice and congratulatory messages to that specific winner. These emails can be customized to give a personal touch, and finally sent to the winners. The choice totally depends on you; automatic emails are also generated by selling manager as well.

End of auction email

If you like to send automated emails to all the bidders informing them about the closing of the current auction, a reliable software can be employed. The software downloads the auction details, generate email, and let you preview the email before sending it out. Many online auction management tools discussed so far have the ability to generate winner confirmatory emails automatically at the end of an auction. If you want to this process, ensure that you enable the feature of preview before the emails are sent.

Inventory records

Many sellers depend on the usual notebook method; crossing off products as they are sold. But a large inventory is usually difficult to manage. Therefore, many people rely on excel spreadsheets to keep track of their inventory. Most of the auction-management suites discussed in this chapter handle inventory for you. Some automatically deduct an item from inventory when you launch an auction. You have your choice of handling inventory directly on your computer or keeping your inventory online with a service that's accessible from any computer, wherever you are. You can also handle your inventory on your desktop through QuickBooks. When you buy merchandise to sell, simply post the bill to QuickBooks, it automatically puts the merchandise into inventory. Afterward, when you input your sale, it deducts the items sold from standing inventory. You can also print a status report whenever you need to view the details of the inventory.

Composing HTML

Fancy auctions look attractive, but that doesn't necessarily mean that your products are going to sell well. The real success lies in competitive prices and reasonable shipping rates. That is because eBay offers a compare items feature to the customers. As far as the decoration is concerned, many auction management tools may assist you in this regard. Many pictures (backgrounds and animations) could be added to your auctions. However, simple HTML doesn't slow up the loading of your page.

This can be done by repeatedly incorporating two or three simple HTML templates, cutting and pasting new text as necessary. Most auction management programs offer you several template choices. The best idea is to stick with a few that are similar, giving a standardized look to your listings, which is just the way major companies give a standardized look to their advertising and identity. Your customers will get used to the look of your auctions and feel comfortable each time they come back to you.

Scheduling listings for bulk upload

In order to launch listings without your presence, and also avoiding the eBay's fees, you should seek help from an online auction management tool. On the other hand, if you can manage it manually, simply use the eBay's Turbo Lister application.

Hosting photos

If all you need is photo hosting, and you've checked out your ISP, but they don't give you any free Web space to use, you can always use eBay's Picture Services to host an extra picture in each auction for some additional fee.

Checking out

When someone wins or buys an item, eBay's checkout integrates directly with PayPal. If you're closing less than 100 auctions a day, that's all you need. EBay and PayPal will also send an e-mail to you and the buyer so that you can arrange for payment. A personalized winner's notification e-mail can easily contain a link to your PayPal payment area, making a checkout service unnecessary.

Printing shipping labels

Printing shipping labels without printing postage can turn out be an arduous work for you. If you are looking to complete this task in one step, two companies, Endicia and PayPal can help you in this regard as they can print your labels and postage all in one step. EBay's Selling Manager print your winner's address label without postage. That works well if you don't mind carrying your packages to the post office for postage.

Tracking buyer information

Tracking buyer information doesn't involve rocket science. Whenever a customer wins an auction or buys items from your 'Buy it Now' feature you get his/her personal information such as name, address, phone number or email. This information could be stored in excel or word. However, if you are looking to involve an auction management service, make sure that you download your data periodically. This is to make your end safe in case you and the online service part ways someday.

Customized Reports

Sales reports, ledgers, and tax information are all significant reports that you should have in your business. Online services and software can provide these reports with different arrangements and style. For instance, PayPal allows you to download your sales data into a format compatible with QuickBooks, a highly reliable and popular bookkeeping program. You can also choose to download your data in Excel spreadsheet format. PayPal reports are full of intensely detailed information about your sales and deposits. Putting this information in a standard accounting software program on a regular basis makes your yearly calculations easier to digest.

Submitting feedback

If you're running a lot of listings, leaving feedback for all of them takes a huge effort. One solution is to automate the submission of feedback through an online service such as eBay's Selling Manager Pro. But it is very difficult to synchronize the timings of the feedback. Don't leave feedback for an eBay transaction before you hear back from the buyer that the purchase is reasonable. Leaving positive feedback immediately after you've received payment from the buyer is too soon. The feedback should be forwarded after you receive an e-mail that confirms the satisfaction of the customer.

Bonding- Making your business safe

Everyone is familiar with the intensity of competition on eBay. The sellers are always thriving for new techniques to entice the customers. New surfers arrive at eBay's site with three different predetermined concepts in mind. Some assume they are going to have fun and find unique products. Some others think they might get a hand to an exciting offer. While some others a bit hesitant think they may catch themselves in a fraudulent scheme. For sellers on eBay, the last kind of surfers is a real pain. Obviously, the sellers have worked their hearts out to make a name on eBay. How can they let that happen? You can counter the public's misconception about the dishonest eBay sellers in two ways: either by getting a SquareTrade seal or by getting your listings bonded through buySAFE. These two programs will ensure a safe business between you and your customer, and it will also help you avoid getting negative feedback.

Bonding your sales with buySAFE

In the past, escrow.com was the only option for the sellers on eBay. Whenever large transactions were there, they have to indulge escrow (a third party for the safety of payment and products) to satisfy the buyers. However, there was a drawback associated with it; the sellers were not able to withdraw their money until the security period is terminated. That seriously hindered the cash flow, and the sellers were finding it difficult to manage. Lately, there have been many scandals in the online escrow too. Swindlers put up sham Web sites, offer expensive items for sale online, and then run the escrow through their bogus site. The buyer, thinking everything is legit, releases their money. After the money arrives, however, the Web site is taken down, the bad guys disappear with the money. From then, escrow has gotten a bad reputation with buyers. Finally, there are some practical alternatives. Something to cheer about both for the customers and the sellers.

What is bonding?

A bond guarantees that the person involved in the contract will stick to all of the promises he made. That is, the product will be sold exactly as it was advertised. A bond ensures that the buyer will not incur a financial loss. On the contrary, bonding is the only licensed and regulated form of seller guarantee. The buySAFE company is an eBay certified developer. They also involve Liberty Mutual (one of America's largest financial services provider) to bond eBay sellers' transactions. The bond will ensure the safety of the customers and will refund the money or replace the item if the seller doesn't stick to the promises he made.

The bond can protect buyers in the following ways. The bonded seller fails to deliver the product to the buyer. The seller delivers a different product that doesn't meet the criteria of the descriptions and pictures on eBay. The seller offers a return policy but refuses to implement it. The seller sent the product through different shipping method, and the item arrives broken (when the buyer has paid for the insurance, but the seller fails to insure the product). The seller refuses to follow the payment policy described in the listing.

Bonding your auctions give the customer a sigh of relief; they will feel more confident, and you can expect more order from them in future. These bonds are assuring your safety as well. Additionally, you will get the payments fast. However, bonding is not just restricted to large transactions. Many small setup holders are also employing them in their businesses, and their sales are growing too. When you bond your items, a seal is displayed, and when a potential buyer clicks that seal, they will be directed to a page that elaborates what it is about.

How to bond on eBay?

Getting your items bonded on eBay is a straightforward and simple task. But in order to get the facility of bonding on eBay, you need to fulfill some requirements. You should have an eBay rating of 100, your feedback should be 98 percent positive, and you should be making $1000 a month to qualify.

If you fulfill those requirements, you then fill out a form on the buySAFE Web site, which asks you information about yourself and your business. After applying, you undergo a thorough qualification process that evaluates your online sales experience and reputation; verifies your identity; and analyzes your financial stability. Then you must also legally commit to either honoring their terms of sale or repaying any losses that you may inflict. Yes, you may have great feedback, but bonding is not about the people who are already buying from you. The point is to attract new buyers with a guarantee that *proves* you're professional and unshakable.

What happens when something advances the way you didn't anticipate?

If a transaction advances the way you didn't desire, don't worry, the customer is still there, you can discuss the matter. If the customer contacts buySAFE, he/she is directly sent back to you. If for some reason, the customer still insists on help resolving the issue, he or she may fill out a problem transaction report on the buySAFE Web site. The report states the problem and what the seller can do to resolve the issue. On your Seller Services page, you'll see a red View Problem button. By clicking it the Problem Summary page is viewed, and then the Problem button is clicked to see the buyer's viewpoint. E-mail is sent to you, and your response is recorded. If nothing has been solved after two e-mail exchanges, a professional mediator (a claims representative) joins in to bury the hatchet.

The mediation process doesn't charge a fee from any party. The mediator may contact both the buyer and seller to get both sides of the story. A bond from a warranty company, such as Liberty Mutual, is a legal obligation to protect both parties. The bond protects the seller from false accusations and the buyer from losing his or her money. If no compromise happens, the mediator is bound to make a mandatory decision, based on the evidence provided, in favor of either party. Liberty Mutual is controlled by each state's insurance department and is held accountable by them for scrutinizing each claim.

CHAPTER SIX
GETTING STARTED WITH YOUR EBAY STORE

If your business is doing well on eBay, it is better to open a store on eBay. An eBay store is totally inclined towards the Buy it Now feature; all items are set at a fixed-price and persist on the eBay's site until canceled or listed for at least 30 days. The whole idea behind opening an eBay store is to practice the freedom of Buy it Now feature. Opening an eBay Store can expand your business. EBay is emphasizing the fixed-price format, and buyers are also looking forward towards that format. eBay stores are very popular nowadays, and almost every known brand has opened a store on eBay. An eBay Store provides you a platform where you can run your business independently; communicating and dealing with customers directly. But eBay Stores are not a complete remedy if you are not willing to put in the extra effort.

Most of the people do not enjoy success with the eBay stores, and that's not because opening an eBay store is a bad idea, but running an eBay Store demands increased amount of dedication and exertion. No matter how many money-back guarantees you get from online spammers promising fairy-tale accomplishment on eBay, the only magic is composing yourself and getting started with hard work as soon as possible. Obviously, it is not easy to bring customers to your store. If you're just beginning on eBay, the best thing is to postpone the idea of opening an eBay Store until your feedback rating is over 100. It's all about experience, and a person learns from experiences. Taking part in transactions on eBay is a great practice because you will be able to see mistakes that sellers make when they sell to you. Some sellers will send you e-mails using hostile tone, and you'll have a true understanding of how quality customer service will help you build your business. You'll also learn from your own mistakes and be able to provide better service to your customers.

Eligibility criteria of opening a store

If you're ready to take your business to the next level and are determined enough; let's plunge deep to get some information about the eligibility criteria of opening a store. Following are the requirements that should be met before opening an eBay's store.

- **Registered seller:** You should be a registered seller on the eBay site with valid credit information on record.

- **Feedback rating:** You must have a feedback rating of 20 or higher, and your ID must be verified. However, a

PayPal account with valuable transactions is also necessary for a longer run. You can also qualify without the 20 feedback rating if your ID is verified. But you really won't have enough experience to run your store without that valuable feedback. In reality, these supplementary prerequisites help to gain more achievements.

- **PayPal account:** You should possess a business or premier (personal) PayPal account. In order to accept credit cards, your PayPal account must be verified. You should be familiar of the necessity of accepting credit cards. It is vital for building sales, and also PayPal is widely accepted by buyers. Make sure that you completely understand the working of a PayPal account. It will help you make up your mind about the types of payments you will accept, in case you allow transactions from different countries.

- **Sales experience:** The minimal transaction requirement of 20 must be met, but you should have selling and buying experience over and above the 20 transactions required by eBay; it will surely pay you back. Undoubtedly, experience always remains the biggest thing to count on.

- **Stock:** Initiating an eBay store without sufficient stock in hand is not a great idea. You must have enough stock so that the sales remain consistent. Furthermore, if you buy in bulk quantity, you will get much lower prices.

- **Devotion:** Devotion is the key to success. You should spare time at least once a day to check out your eBay business, and the shipping details of the bought inventory in a swift manner. Keep in mind that the items you listed as store inventory will not come up in an eBay search unless eBay can come up with thirty or less of the item searched for. The only way new buyers can find your store inventory is by clicking the Find Items in eBay Stores tab in eBay search bar, by searching items on the store hub page, or by clicking from one of your auction pages to see what else you have on sale.

Types of Stores

All eBay stores compete on the same level. It means that all the stores are equally searchable as far as the eBay stores hub page is concerned. In fact, you are competing with the big brands on the identical level. All eBay stores have some things in common, although the difference of subscription charges is always there. Following options are identical in all eBay stores.

- **Listings:** All your eBay listings, whether fixed price, auction or store merchandise will be presented in your eBay store.

- **Specific URL:** Your eBay store has a specific URL. This Internet address can be used for promotional purposes if you are looking to promote your store.

- **Search box:** When the customers visit your store, they will be able to search through your inventory with the aid of a search box. The customers will put the item title they are looking for in the search box, and all your inventory will be automatically searched.

- **Cross promotions:** For sale on the regular eBay site, you can always embed thumbnail promotions for your store products within each of your products.

- **Reports:** On a monthly basis you will receive seller reports on your sales through email.

eBay stores are divided into three levels viz. the basic, premium, and anchor. These stores can be rented for different subscription charges. The stores can be rented for a monthly subscription fee or yearly subscription fee. You can opt either one of them depending on your business and budget. The basic store can be rented for $24.95 per month (monthly subscription fee), and $19.95 per month (yearly subscription fee). The premium store can be rented for $74.95 per month (monthly subscription fee), and $59.95 per month (yearly subscription fee). The anchor store can be rented for $349.95 per month (monthly subscription fee), and $299.95 per month (yearly subscription fee). There is no limit to the number of products you can enlist on your store irrespective of the store type you choose. Most of the power sellers go for the basic store as it can fulfill their demands. Interestingly, a customer by no means can assess whether you have a basic, premium, or anchor store. So it is a clever move to stick to the basic store. The design of the store is completely up to you; customizable and editable. You can customize it according to your preferences.

Picking up your store name

You've decided to delve and open an eBay Store. Did you come up with a decent name for your store? Your store name doesn't need to be corresponding your eBay user ID, but they're more noticeable if they relate to each other. You can use your company name, your business name, or a name that describes your business. It is better to pick the identical name for your eBay Store that you are going to use in all your online businesses. In this manner, you'll instigate to create an identity in the form of a brand that customers will come to recognize and rely upon. Your online eBay Store should not substitute your Web site; it should be an extension of it. When people shop at your eBay Store, you should avail that opportunity and make them customers of your Web site through your store's About the Seller page. This page is the same as the About Me page on eBay.

Setting up shop

With all the introductory information you have, now let's move to set up your store. Navigate through the site map to find the eBay stores hub page and click the 'open a store' option. This will direct you to the seller's hub of eBay stores, and you will find some promotional stuff relating to opening a store by courtesy of eBay. You are already familiar with that kind of information so you can skip that part, but don't forget to check the policy changes as they may affect your store's operation. Before hitting the tab that leads to opening your store, ask yourself two questions.

Am I determined enough to open an eBay store? Opening a store is sheer commitment. It won't do any good if you are not going to put in the extra effort. You should have inventory to fill it and the determination to add more products to your listings. Your store is a daily obligation. If you have planned a vacation, be sure to accommodate a substitute who can carry on your work; shipping is the main concern. You simply can't leave a store on its own just like any physical store. Otherwise, your customers will find some other merchandise to shop from. Nevertheless, eBay also provides an exciting store's vacation feature which can be used to let the customers know you are on a temporary break until a specified date.

Am I willing to work against all the odds? You have to be prepared for times when you are not feeling well, but the orders still need to be delivered. It is part of the commitment; you have to deliver the shipments at any cost. EBay has only provided you a platform to exhibit your merchandise, but the success can only be achieved by hard labor. If you are committed enough to fulfill these responsibilities, continue to read to explore further.

Subscribing to stores

As you are always logged in on your computer, Open a Store tab will direct you to subscribe the eBay stores page. The same agreement page will pop up which you had seen while making an account initially on eBay. The getting started process is easy. Select the type of store, and the basic store is the most promising choice to make as discussed earlier. Next, comes the title (name) of your store, type in the name of your store. Your eBay store name can't exceed the 35 characters limit. Before submitting your store's name, be sure that you are not infringing someone else's copyrights or trademarks. You are also not allowed to use any variation of eBay's present trademarks in your store's name. The basic store comes with free selling manager and sales report plus. However, the selling manager pro is free with the premium and anchor levels. Once all the details are put in, finally hit the subscribe button to get started. As soon as you click the subscribe button, the clock begins to tick on your monthly fees. Don't press the subscribe button if you are not going to start immediately. They will start billing the moment you hit the subscribe button; it is better to get some vital information before really getting started. Go to the Stores design page, and follow these guidelines.

On the design page, first, choose a color theme. EBay provides some fascinating color and graphic themes with 14 clearly organized layouts, but the color scheme can be changed to get stunning combinations. Select the colors that are easy on the eyes and avoid using vibrant and sharp colors. The colors that are easy on eyes give a comfortable selling environment as the surfers can easily navigate through your web store. In case you don't like any of their themes, you can also design your own customized theme.

You should also come up with an exciting idea about your store's logo. The creation of a logo is a necessity; you simply can't ignore it; gives a unique touch to your business. Utilizing eBay's clip art to make a logo gives an unprofessional look to your business. A basic logo is created without much panic, you can also hire someone to do this task, and it won't cost you much.

After finalizing your theme, step towards the description of your store. Type in a short description of your store, short because you can't exceed the 300-word limit. The description needs to be electrifying covering almost every aspect of your merchandise. You can't incorporate links within your text so try to find some impactful words to fill that space. The description is immensely vital. The keyword information you put here is used as a reference whenever customers search eBay stores. To make your store look more appealing add a graphic (eBay's clip art style banner or you can also use a customizable one) to your store. With that, the process of opening a store is completed. Your store is live and ready to make sales when you fill in the listings. Congratulations! EBay automatically fits you in the right category, if you are dealing in products from two different categories they will enlist you in both categories.

Running your store

You can customize and edit your store's interface by clicking the Manage your Store tab at the bottom of your store's page.

Store design and marketing

The store editing tab is further divided into the following sub-tabs.

Store builder

This tab takes you to your original store setup region. You can edit the name, theme, and description of your store here. You can also change the way your items are displayed in the listings. There are two presentations: the gallery or list view. The gallery view should be preferred over the list view because the items are enlarged and more visible than the list view. Another important aspect is the way items are sorted. The items can be sorted according to lowest priced first, highest priced first, newest arrivals that are according to date of the listings, or items that will be ending first.

Custom pages

Most successful sellers on eBay have the privilege to use a store policy page. EBay supplies a wide range of templates when you are going to set up a policy page. Just click the Create new Page tab to see the range of layouts. The page should be filled using HTML, but don't panic if you don't know HTML because eBay assists you with an easy to use HTML generator. You may wonder which things to add to the policy page; following are some important pointers that should be there.

First, the shipping locations should be vividly explained. If you are not going to ship the products overseas, it is better to mention it. Second, specify the sales tax you are going to collect. If your state doesn't need you to collect sales tax, leave that portion blank. In case your state allows to collect the tax, mention your state's policy on sales tax. Most of the states won't permit you to accumulate the sales tax unless the product is shipped in your home state. Third, ensure that you mention your customer service and return policy. Provide relevant information about the refund and exchange policies. All other relevant information that suits your business should be added. You can also set up a custom home page for your store, but this isn't a good choice. It is better to land the customer directly to your store's home page.

Custom categories

This tab will give a personal touch to your store. You may name up to 300 custom categories relevant to the products you sell on your store.

Custom listing header

The custom listing header display is one of the best tools you can use to bring folks into your store. Hit the tab and select the option to display your custom listing header on all your eBay auctions and fixed-price sales. This will boost customers to visit your eBay Store when they browse your eBay listings. When customizing, be sure to include your store logo as well as a store search box. You can see how the store header looks at the top of an eBay listing.

Promotions

EBay has added some exciting promotional features for eBay store holders. These promotional features are only supplied to the store owners, and the most splendid tool is the cross-promotion box which is a freebie. In normal setting or the usual eBay's seller account, the cross-promotion box is only visible when a customers buy a product from the seller regardless of the auction or fixed price format. On the contrary, a registered eBay store holder gets the facility of cross-promotion box twice. Firstly when the product is bought and an additional with the regular listings. They can also select which items are shown with the individual auctions. The cross-promotions can be set up to show other items from related store categories. The selection of items to place in the cross-promotions box could either be set by default or be done manually.

Making a sale

From a buyer's perspective, eBay store shopping is a different experience. As mentioned before eBay stores deal in a fixed-price format so the customers get the product as soon as you can ship it. On the other hand, the customers participating in an auction would have to wait for the auction to run its course. Even though your auctions are displayed on your store's home page, all regular listings are integrated with 'Buy it Now' feature. This is how the sales process flows through the customer's end.

The buyer clicks the buy it now button and the review payments page pops up. This page contains a review of their purchase along with the shipment amount you specified on your item. The buyer then fills in the shipping information you need, and eBay's notification only arrives when the customer has filled in all the details for you. Finally, the customer confirms the transaction, and both the parties (you and the customer) receive emails from eBay about the sales confirmation.

Your eBay store is a crucial backup to your auctions. It is also a great place to put out of season items. The subscription charges of an eBay store are covered with only a few sales, and once you have established your store, you will see big bucks rolling.

CHAPTER SEVEN

BECOMING A POWER SELLER

While browsing through items on eBay, you might have caught a glimpse of Power Seller badge adjacent to a member's user identification. The eBay Power seller status is given only to those sellers who sustain impeccable professionalism on the site. EBay refers power sellers as 'pillar of the community.' Power sellers have to maintain certain monthly goals of gross merchandise sales (GMS). In simple words, they have to keep the money flowing through the sales of their products. Obviously, they earn this status by providing prime quality products and exceptional customer service. You may have noticed many sellers with tons of feedback on their profile, but they still lack the power seller status. This doesn't necessarily mean that they are bad sellers, it's just that some of their transactions might haven't gone ideally and resulted in negative feedback. That is why it is vital to go through the feedback and policies of the seller before evaluating their performance. Most of the times buyer neglect the seller's policies before making a purchase and then end up giving them negative feedback which is detrimental to the seller's profile and business.

Eligibility criteria of a Power Seller

In order to become a power seller on eBay, you must fulfill the following requirements.

- You should be an active eBay seller for at least 90 days

- Sell a minimum of $1,000 in sales or 100 items per month, for three successive months or a minimum average of items sold on the site per month for the past three months

- Sell a minimum of $12,000 or 1,200 items for the previous twelve months

- Have a minimum overall feedback rating of 100

- Maintain at least a 98 feedback percentage

- Keep your eBay account current

- Conform to all eBay policies

- Maintain a rating of 4.5 or higher for the past 12 months in all four Detailed Seller Ratings (DSRs)

- Run your business by safeguarding eBay's community values. eBay sends you a notification when you qualify. If you feel you have qualified and may have unintentionally deleted the e-mail, find the Power Seller's page from the Site Map tab and try to log in.

Power Seller Tiers

Becoming a power seller gives you access to an exclusive eBay's community. The community has five tiers of membership viz. the bronze, silver, gold, platinum, and titanium. The tiers categorization depends on the monthly sales. Each power seller tier provides the seller with extraordinary privileges. One of the most promising benefits is the ability of the power seller to contact the customer support program of eBay when an issue needs to be addressed. The customer support is divided into three discrete segments such as the email and chat facility, phone call facility, and account management facility.

To be eligible for the bronze tier, you should sell a minimum of $1,000 or 100 items in the following month. As a reward, you will get 24 hours facility of email and chat, 6am-10pm phone call facility, but you will not get any account management help from eBay.

To be eligible for silver tier, you should sell a minimum of $3,000 or 300 items in the following month. As a reward, you will get 24 hours facility of email and chat, 6am-10pm phone call facility, but you will not get any account management help from eBay.

To be eligible for the gold tier, you should sell a minimum of $10,000 or 1000 items in the following month. As a reward, you will get 24 hours facility of email and chat, 24-hour phone call facility, and you will also get some partial provision regarding account management help from eBay.

To be eligible for the platinum tier, you should sell a minimum of $25,000 or 2500 items in the following month. As a reward, you will get 24 hours facility of email and chat, 24/7 phone call facility, and you will also get full provision regarding account management help from eBay.

To be eligible for titanium tier, you should sell a minimum of $150,000 or 15,000 items in the following month. As a reward, you will get 24 hours facility of email and chat, 24-hour phone call facility, and you will also get full provision regarding account management help from eBay.

Perks of being a Power Seller

Besides the customer support, power seller gets access to a secretive community within the eBay's site that is strictly reserved for the power sellers. This area is password protected, and only power seller can truly access it. The power seller's newsgroup, power seller's discussion board, and access to special items on eBay are some of the exciting privileges. eBay has officially admitted that the power sellers give customers the buying experience. They have devised a plan to pay the power sellers back by providing them some valuable benefits.

Enhanced visibility in search results

The search results listings are arranged according to the seller's potential of buyer satisfaction. Obviously, the sellers with the highest level of buyer satisfaction are placed at the top of the table. In terms of eBay, sellers with detailed seller ratings (DSRs) above 4.7 for the past 30 days will receive 5 to 25 percent more audience exposure than the average seller.

Discounts on final value fees

Discounts have always been a reward, and everyone loves them too. eBay discounts the final value fees in the monthly charge sheet to power sellers who maintain their detailed seller ratings (DSRs). However, you should have a minimum of 4.6 ratings or above to avail the benefit. The discounts on final value fees start at 5% and go up to 20%. The company has divided the discounts percentage into three different categories.

- When you are a Power Seller with all four of your detailed seller ratings over the past 30-days time frame are 4.6 or higher, you qualify for a 5% discount on Final Value Fees.

- When you are a Power Seller with all four of your detailed seller ratings over the past 30-days time frame are 4.8 or higher, you qualify for a 15% discount on Final Value Fees

- When you are a Power Seller with all four of your detailed seller ratings over the past 30-days time frame are 4.9 or higher, you qualify for a 20% discount on Final Value Fees

Health Insurance Facility

Power sellers have the opportunity to buy exclusive health care insurance. This health care facility is not limited to the power sellers alone, the employees and blood relatives of the power seller can also avail the opportunity.

Official Power seller logo

EBay provide power sellers with amazing templates for their customized business cards and stationary. They also give an official consent to use the power seller logo.

Discount on upgrades

Besides the discount on final value fee and listing credits, power sellers also get credit for any listing upgrade fees. For instance, the upgrades such as bold, subtitle, and all that extra kind of stuff.

Reseller marketplace

One of the most lucrative benefits of a power seller is the entry in the reseller marketplace. eBay runs a special website for power sellers that sells liquidation and wholesale stocks to power sellers. A 4.6 percentage average DSR rating implies that you form the top 50 percent of sellers when talking in terms of buyer satisfaction. Undoubtedly, becoming a power seller is a foremost step to eBay's competent environment.

CHAPTER EIGHT
SUCCESS TIPS FOR SELLING ON EBAY

Now that we have spent some time looking at the basics of setting up your account and getting started with your first listing, it is time to get down to work and really start to understand what selling on eBay is all about. This chapter is going to look at some of the tips and tricks that you should try out when you are ready to start selling for profit on eBay.

Listings

Let's take a look at listings first. Listings are the way that you offer your products for sale and make money so doing them the proper way is so important. You need to make sure that the listings are looking nice, with some great pictures and a full description, so that the customers will be drawn to them and are more likely to make a purchase in your shop compared to the shop of another similar product. Some of the tips that you can try out to make your listings shine and to get them to stand out in the crowd include:

- Remember the buyers when you are creating the listing. When writing the listing, think of what you would like to see or know in a listing before you make a purchase and then add this information in.

- Put the reserve price in the details of the listing. This helps the customer to know how high they will have to bid and can save them some time. If your reserve bid is more than they want to spend on the item, they will move on, but if it is low enough, they will perhaps start bidding a bit higher, bringing you a bit more profit.

- Provide accurate costs of shopping. Buyers may not know the exact shipping price all the time, but they can usually tell when it is too high. To protect your seller reputation, find out how much it will be to ship the item and or get a postal scale to help you get the best estimation.

- Use USPS shipping boxes—you can get these for free from eBay if you live in the United States. If you plan to sell some larger items, these will really help you out. While you will still need to pay for shipping the item, you get the supplies for free which can save you a lot.

- Pick out the right length of time for the auction. You can choose between 1, 3, 5, 7, and 10 days when setting the auction and each item is going to need a different amount of time to get the item sold. For items that are high selling, for example, 1-day auctions are the best because they will rank higher and many people don't want to wait around to see how the price goes.

- Choose when to post the listing—the most popular time to end your posting is on a Sunday evening around 8 p.m. PST, so no matter what time you choose your listing for, make sure it ends on that day.

- Be careful with brand names in the listings—this has caused some issues on eBay. For example, if you use Chanel, you will be flagged for keyword spamming and even copyright infringement.

- Check out the listing before posting it—this helps you to make sure that there aren't any mistakes, such as punctuation or grammar so that the listing looks great.

- Create the listings in batches—sometimes it can take a lot of time to post new products on eBay. Instead of doing each listing at a time, consider doing a batch of them. If they are similar items, you will be able to save some time and get through the process a bit faster. It keeps the flow going in between tasks and prevents you from wasting too much time.

- Avoid negative terms—there are some sellers who will use negative terms in their listings. These may seem like a way to protect yourself, such as "Don't bid if you are not planning to pay" but they are also going to scare a lot of bidders away. They don't want to deal with someone who is so difficult and will pick another product.

Picking the right price

Pricing can be an important part of whether a customer is going to choose your product over another one. Of course, you want to make as much money from the product as possible, but you also have to pick a price that will entice the customer to pick you over someone else. Some of the things that you should consider when it comes to picking the right price includes:

- When you purchase a wholesale good, make sure that you can double your price. Go with products that you can purchase in bulk since this lowers the price while increasing your revenue. You may need to check the eBay Sold Listings part and see how much other items are selling for to see if it's right for you.

- When selling a popular product, go with a lower starting price. This helps bidders to place higher bids in the beginning and over time, they may bid higher than other products because they want to "win."

- Use the "What's It Worth?" feature on eBay. This offers you a free 7-day trial and can help you out when picking out competitive prices for your items. If you want to grow your business on eBay, this tool may be worth your time.

- Consider the shipping—if you are selling an expensive product on this site, consider offering free shipping to the customer. This can help to increase your chances of making a sale.

Customer Service

Any time that you sell a product to someone else, they are going to be looking to see how your customer service is to help them determine if they will choose you or another company to purchase from. You need to be able to provide some of the best customer service possible to win out in the end. Professional language, prompt responses to questions, and fast delivery can all help to increase your customer service. Some of the things that you should do to provide good customer service to your buyers include:

- Listen to the customers—if your customers have sent over questions about your items, take the time to read through the messages and respond. If there are issues they are worried about with the product, respond back honestly to help build up trust with the buyer.

- Deal with negative feedback—no one wants to receive negative feedback, but there are going to be times when a customer is not that happy with your work. First, never retaliate against these; it may make you feel better, but it will make you as a professional look bad. When you get this negative feedback, you can message the buyer or reply to the feedback directly. Ask how you could rectify the situation, but if the buyer doesn't respond, just move on and don't worry about it.

- Give the buyers feedback—you don't need to write out something specific for every buyer you work with; create some feedback that you can store on your computer to just copy and paste to save time. Don't wait to hear back from the buyer, or you may be waiting a long time. If you already got paid for the purchase, go ahead and leave the feedback.

- Add a thank you note to the packages. This is a nice personal touch that can make the customer feel special.

- Offer discounts on shipping—if your customer is going to purchase a few products from you, you could offer a discount on the shipping to help entice them. Depending on the size of the products, you should be able to send them in the flat rate boxes from USPS so you will get a discount that you can pass on to the customer.

Customer service is probably one of the most important things that you can work on. Sure a nice listing and some good keywords in the title are important, but you do need to make sure that you are treating your customers nicely. If they feel that you are rude or unprofessional, they will just go to one of the other many options for sellers that are on eBay, and you are sure to get bad reviews as well so that you start to lose on customers and can't make any money. Be professional, keep your promises, and don't overcharge the customers and you should be just fine with this.

Being organized as a seller on eBay

While selling on eBay can be a great way to make some extra money and earn a living, it is important that you have some organizational skills in play. If you are bad at organizing your information or getting things done, eBay may not be the right choice for you to go with. On the other hand, if you are good at keeping up with stuff, like to meet a challenge, and want to make money in your own free time, eBay can be great. Here are some of the things that you can do to make sure that your eBay store is organized and you are getting the best out of all your work.

- Have an office space—this can help you keep organized because all of your products, packaging materials, computer, and the printer will be in one place. It prevents anything from getting lost and helps you to have your own little space that no one else is able to mess with.

- Avoid shipping each day—you don't want to waste time and energy going to the post office each day. Choose a few days a week that you will ship out and then send all of your products out and let your customers know this. Another idea is to schedule your pickups so that USPS or another company will come to your home and actually take the deliveries for you.

- Keep track of your money—a spreadsheet is a good place to start with this. Write down the fees, expenses, and your earnings each month to keep things organized. This helps you to see if you need to make some changes to the process you use. It can also be helpful when you are getting ready to work on your taxes at the end of the year since it will all be in one place.

Keep up with the trends

It is amazing at how quickly the trends on eBay and other sites will change. Something that was selling well a week ago will now be one of the lowest sellers, and you need to keep up with this to ensure that you are going to continue making a profit from this work. If you want to keep this going as a stream of income, make sure that you keep track of how the trends are doing each week or so. Some of the places you can look in order to learn the new trends for selling include:

- EBay top selling items—there is a page on eBay you can visit that will list which items are selling the best online. This is a great place to start when looking at trends and trying to decide what you would like to sell.

- Magazines and newspapers—not only can you keep up with your news and entertainment, but you can keep track of which items are really good sellers for you to work with.

- Television—take a look at the commercials surrounding your favorite show, and you are sure to see a lot of products that are really popular at the time.

- Radio—this is another good place to start for finding trends. Listen to some of the most popular stations to have an idea of which products they are promoting.

How to increase your profits

While it may take a bit to learn how to make profits with your eBay store, it will happen for you if you keep working, finding good products, and pricing the items just right. Plus eBay provides you with lots of options to make money, including options that are outside of eBay but are partnered with eBay, which can help you to increase your income. Some of the best ways to work with eBay and increase your earnings, even more, include:

- Expand out. EBay has another site called Half.com which is a program that is used for games, textbooks, books, and movies. If you want to sell some of your old media products or books, you can expand out to Half.com rather than just selling on eBay. This increases your audience and makes it easier for sale.

- Sell items that are seasonal. Christmas is a good example of this. People are always looking for good products to purchase as gifts during this time, and if you can offer a discount on them, you can make a lot of sales during this time. Last minute gifts, seasonal items, and more do really well on eBay.

- Sell products overseas. If you are willing to send items overseas, you could tap into a big market. Many name brand items aren't available in other countries so if you are willing to get these items and sell and ship them to other customers who are overseas.

- Revamp your product presentation—this includes making your listing look as amazing as possible. Invest in a good camera to take some pictures, pick out good product titles with the right keywords, link your products together to customers will go over to them to make other purchases and fill out your profile information including a cover photo and an about me section to add some trust in the market.

- Use some social media—social media is one of the best ways to get customers, whether you are looking for some that are local or overseas. Pinterest is a great way to show off some of your products but talking on Facebook and Twitter, as well as a few others, to increase your online presence and to make it easier for customers to find you.

Key Principles to make more Profit

Your efforts should be focused on earning money as soon as possible. It is always better to earn money on your own rather than borrowing the startup capital. There are three key principles that will help you become profitable. The profit can come in the first place or you to have to wait until your business grows. We will look at these principles with real case studies, so you can have a better idea of comprehending them and eventually implementing them into your life. Incorporating these fundamental principles can make your business grow with an increased profit. These three principles are as follows:

1.   Pricing the product/service in terms of the benefits it provides rather than the cost of its production.

2.   Customers should be offered a (limited) range of prices.

3.   Earn more than once for the same thing.

These three principles will make your business more profitable for sure. Now it's time to study each of them separately.

Principle 1: Base Prices in relation to Benefits, Not Expenditures

Before understanding the principle, it is better to have a concept of feature and benefit. These two characteristics are somewhat different. A feature is a description of the product and service. For example, "This dress fit well and look amazing," whereas a benefit is a value someone receives from the product or service under consideration like, "This dress make you feel healthy and attractive." People usually tend towards features and talk about them, but since most purchases involve emotional decisions, it is much more persuasive to discuss benefits of the product/service.

As you emphasize on the benefits of your offering rather than the features, in the same way, you should base the price of your offer on the benefits rather than the actual production cost or the time you spent creating it. In fact, a completely wrong way to decide on the pricing is to think about how much time it took you to

produce it or how much your time is worth.

When you base your prices on the benefits, be prepared for the attack because many people will criticize you on raising the price so high regardless of your product/service. Almost everyone struggles in their new business because of offering the lowest price. Of course, what works for Walmart probably won't work for everyone. In fact, very few businesses sustain on such a tight budget strategy, therefore competing on value is much better and fruitful.

Alan Jeff, the agent who helps busy people book their vacations, charges a flat rate of $500 for his services. Sometimes it takes him a fair amount of time to research and book the trip, but on some occasions, he gets lucky, and it can take as little as two to three minutes of research and a short phone call. Alan is sure that people don't care about the time it takes for him to accomplish the task, and they are actually paying him for his expertise on booking vacations and trips. As a whole, the time cost of Alan is variable, but on an average, it takes him 30 to 35 minutes per booking. The benefit which he provides is first-class and business-class tickets for worldwide vacations, and the cost of his service doesn't vary with time.

Jim Hall, a stationary guy who sells daily use stationary products on eBay, creates lovely Christmas greeting cards that are mostly sold in bulk. A single copy is available, but many people prefer a bundle of five or ten. The materials cost him $4.5 each, and the benefit it provides is the nicely designed cards that can be sent to close friends and family members during the Christmas vacations. It cost $17.55 to the buyers, and most promisingly, it is not directly related to the cost of the materials.

Some examples are even more extreme when it comes to profit, especially in selling instructional and informational products. Every day the countless amount of money is spent on courses that cost virtually nothing to distribute. As all the costs were in developmental and initial marketing. So when you are thinking about the pricing of a new project, ask yourself questions like, "How will this idea improve the quality of my customers' lives, and what should be the worth of that improvement in them?" After considering all these aspects, set your price accordingly, while still being clear in your mind that your offer is giving your customers the right value for their money.

Principle 2: Propose a (limited) range of prices

Selecting an initial price according to the benefits of the product/service is the most vital principle to ensure profitability. But in a good business model, you should be looking for the optimal profitability. To build more cushion into your business model, you have to present more than one price for your offer. This practice typically has a huge impact on your business growth as it allows you to increase the income without increasing your customer base. For instance, you are selling a product, the same product (in this case an e-book) can be priced differently. But you may be wondering how it is possible? Let's make it possible then. The same e-book can be sold as the paperback version or narrated version. Obviously, the narrated version is more expensive than the paperback version, but you can demand more. It also gives the customer an additional option to choose according to his/her comfort.

Let's look at this principle in a bigger context. Consider Apple, which famously produces products and doesn't even bother to compete on price. Regardless of their products quantity, there is always a fascinating array of products and prices. You can buy anything from mid- levels to more expensive products for super users tagged as the high-end version. This array of options let them earn much more money than they otherwise would. Companies following the same pattern usually generate more revenue than the companies which are not incorporating this principle into their business. This is probably due to the fact that some people are interested in buying expensive (biggest and best) products, even if the biggest and best is much more expensive than the regular version. These kind of sales are responsible for the overall increase in selling prices.

To get a better idea of this concept, have a look at an example of two pricing options: one offered at a fixed price and another based on the grade/tier structure. It is just an example model, and you can always substitute any prices to check its compatibility with your business.

Option a: The Best Medical Lectures Ever

Price: $250

Option (a) is simple and straightforward as it provides the choice like: Do you want to buy these lectures or not?

Now let's have a look at an alternative idea that is almost always better.

Option b: The Best Medical Lectures Ever

Choose your preferred version option below

Best Medical Lectures Ever, Budget version, $250

Best Medical Lectures Ever, Enhanced version, $ 389

Best Medical Lectures Ever, Premium version, $479

You can feel the difference as the option (b) presents the choice as follows: Which lecture package would like to buy?

There are chances that some people will go for the budget version, some may opt the enhanced version, while some may go for the premium version as well. As far as you don't complicate things, another tier can be added to the top or even the bottom of these grades in the form of the exclusive premium version or the free/trial version respectively.

Now let's look at the difference of revenue generated by these two options. Option (a) with a flat rate of $250 and say 20 sales, the total amount generated is $5000. On the contrary, option (b) with variable rate and 20 sales (supposing 12 choose the middle one, 4 choose budget version, and 4 choose premium version) generates $7584. The total difference between the money generated is $2584, or a $129.2 plus on each sale.

The key to this strategy is to offer a limited range of prices for the customers to make a healthy choice. But do not complicate things as this will confuse the buyer. By providing them with choices, you are not only encouraging them to buy your products but are also enabling them to choose one of the better options that suits them. Different options can be created for different price ranges like Platinum, Gold, and Premium versions. Product plus setup guide (the same thing sold with special guide), and any kind of exclusive or limited quantity selection.

You can also sell the same product at different prices with literally no added features. It's not immoral to sell products like that especially if you are not specifying the additional features. However, it's unethical to sell the same product with different price tags just by adding a sentence like enhanced or upgraded version and in reality adding nothing to it. To reduce confusion, it is better to add something of real value as you upgrade your tier structure.

Principle 3: Get Paid More Than Once

The final strategy to make your business run smoothly generating more profit is to ensure that your payday doesn't come along only once. In fact, you should focus on repeated paydays from the same customers over and over on a regular basis. The terms like continuity program, membership sites, and subscriptions are almost identical. They are roughly the same as they allow you to get paid over and over again by the same customer in favor for ongoing access to a service or the regular delivery of a product.

Referring to the old days when people used to read newspapers (actual paper ones), they would subscribe to have them delivered to their home or office. Presently this subscription stuff is still prevailing but has changed its shape somehow. These days, Netflix offers a subscription to your favorite TV shows and seasons. The utility company has a recurring billing schedule; you use the appliances, and they bill you every month.

Getting paid over and over is actually a big deal if you are considering the two leading advantages it takes along. First, it can bring in a lot of cash, and second, it's a reliable income hardly fluctuated by external factors.

Let's have a look at an example, assuming you offer a subscription service for $15 a month:

50 subscribers at $15 = monthly revenue of $750 or yearly revenue of $9000.

500 subscribers at $15 = monthly revenue of $7,500 or yearly revenue of $90,000.

You can tweak either the number of subscribers or the price of the recurring service to see dramatic improvements.

For instance, adding 50 more subscribers generates $750 more per month or $9000 more per year. Raising the price to $25 a month with a subscriber base of 500 generates $5,000 more per month or $60,000 more per year. Ideally adjusting both options that are attracting more subscribers and raising the price generates an even greater increase.

Note: These numbers may vary, but the important thing to notice is that in almost every case, a recurring billing model always surpasses the single sale model when talking in terms of income generation.

So it is more favorable to attract customers to a recurring model and delivering the best you can to make them feel happy and contented. If you are doing so, you are indeed opening your way for more sales other than the product/service your customers are mostly buying.

Kevin Gentry is an expert at continuity programs. He has built an enormous empire from his art of transforming the one-time buyers to a recurring subscriptions model. Have a look at Kevin's work and the strategies he employed while interacting with customers. His company offers a varied line of complementary products and services. Some of them are one-time purchases that are the source of initiating a new customer relationship, while others are software and hosting services that involve recurring payments either monthly or quarterly. While they strive to build all their product lines, but their general strategy is to transform as many one- time purchase customers as possible to a more remunerative recurring service.

For instance, their StudioPress department sells WordPress themes to online publishers and has over 30,000 customers. These are usually one-time purchases, but many people come back for additional theme purchases. Furthermore, they also provide ongoing support to all of these customers. As time passes, they further offer their SEO service or their new WordPress hosting service to their StudioPress customers, which is a way to make the business long lasting with a specific customer; which both the parties enjoy for an improved mutual beneficial environment. But the main ingredient in their success is the trust they have built from the initial one-time purchase.

Treating the customer with respect is another key principle. It also implies to good behavior even before the initial purchase is made. Kevin and his team provide ample free content and consulting, and once the visitors become customers, the customer service moves one step ahead regardless of the size of the sales. According to Kevin, the key to this model is not market share; instead, it's the share of the customer. He believes to gain more of each customer's budget, and they have to treat every customer as the best customer without any kind of discrimination. And in the process, they end up finding the proverbial "customers for life."

The whole idea behind sharing Kevin's experience and strategies is to get something out of it. The best thing that you should learn from him is his ability and approach on improving his customers' quality of life. Kevin doesn't spend much time worrying about what other people are doing; instead, he spends time on making his customers happy, so they come back to him again and again.

Writing eBay Guides

If you have a talent for writing, this could be a unique way to get yourself recognized through this site. eBay makes it easy for members to write various guides for the community and when you write and publish these guides, you are going to get some fantastic exposure for sellers and buyers alike. Remember that some sellers are also going to want to make purchases later, and if they recognize your name from the guides, they may be more willing to purchase from you.

To write one of these guides, you just need to go into the Guides section of the community and click on "Write your first guide." This will take you to a page where you can pick out the template you want to use for this guide. Pick the one out that you like and then click on "Continue" so that you can go to the editor page and write out the guide.

Don't be scared to write a guide that already has been touched upon. Most people will read a few different guides to learn the information, and you may have a different spin on it that could prove useful to the customer. Some of the topics that you can consider writing about on eBay include:

- How to get started on eBay.

- How to increase your income on eBay

- Information on how to sell in each category

- How to spot a scammer on eBay

- The best tips for sellers on eBay

- The basics of selling on eBay.

In addition to working on a guide with eBay, consider writing in depth reviews of different products. This is going to be located in the same area that the Guides were so it is easy to get started on a review. These reviews may take a bit of time, but they will help to fill out your sellers' page a bit and can make it look complete. It also shows buyers that you have some expertise on a topic and they may be more willing to purchase it from you.

Offer some variety

People shop online because they want to have some variety. They want to see things that they can't get locally, and they want a gift or an item that is unique. If you are selling something like accessories, you may want to include some variety, so the customer has some decisions. You will be able to include some of the different variations in the same posting to offer more options to your customers while reducing how much you pay in listing fees. Don't waste time and money posting them separately; post them together to reduce fees and to make it easier for the customer to see the options that are available for them.

Be careful about words used in posting titles

Words such as amazing, glamorous, and awesome are not good for your title. First, you should let the buyer have a choice on whether this item is awesome or not. Second, when the buyer is doing a search for an item like yours, they won't add these descriptive words to their search. So basically you are just wasting valuable keyword space if you do this. Use keywords that help to describe the product and will help the customer find your product.

Selling products on eBay can be a great way to make an income without wasting your time hoping that someone will find you. If you follow the easy steps in this guidebook, you will find that this process can be easier than ever before.

CONCLUSION

When it comes to finding ways to make extra money for your needs, there can be a lot of options. In most cases, it is going to depend on what you want to do with your time and how much effort you are able to put into the endeavor. Of course, there are a lot of options that may end up being scams or some that will take more time to accomplish than they are worth, but some, such as selling on eBay, can be great ways to make a full time income from this kind of selling.

This guidebook has spent some time looking at why eBay is such a great option for selling your items. You can sell your own personal items to get started and get some experience, or you can choose to go to garage sales and farmers' markets to find some great items at prices low enough for you to make a profit with online. This can be a continuous project, finding new items and posting them for sale again, so eBay makes it easy to turn this into a full time project.

This guidebook has spent time talking about how great eBay is and how you will be able to make some good money simply by listing items and putting them for sale at a good price through eBay. Almost any product will do well with this option as long as you do the process right, although there are some great products that can get you ahead and are easier to sell if you have them. You will learn all the tips and tricks that you need to be successful with eBay and to start bringing in that extra income today.

Free Bonus: Join Our Book Club and Receive Free Gifts Instantly

Click Below For Your Bonus: https://success321.leadpages.co/freebodymindsoul/

Made in the USA
San Bernardino, CA
20 January 2017